Life & Lessons

Latrice Bullock

Presentation by *BookLeaf Publishing*

Web: www.bookleafpub.com

E-mail: info@bookleafpub.com

ISBN: 9789357212977

First edition 2023

I dedicate this book to all my loved ones who can only be reached spiritually. #LU4L

Endure

Life is what you make it they say,
But what if your just trying to make it and life
keeps whipping your ass like a slave,
The smile you force is fake of course,
When your alone with your thoughts, or while
the shower runs hot your eyes release the pain,
The agony of defeat keeps knocking at your
door,
Asking is that enough? Nope she's strong she
can handle more,
Constantly taking and taking till you can no
longer endure,
And your tears are all around and pain drenched
the floor.

Limited Accessibility

I've lost sight of what I thought was right,
Because I love you I give you infinite access to
me and my life,
But if access to you is limited why am I 7/11 to
you and your on mom and pop shop hours to me,
I can't call you when my demons are eating at
my thoughts and the calmness of your "why you
up boo" provides that cushion,
I'm always available when you need but the
reciprocation isn't achieved,
So to save me I must limit me and no I don't feel
bad about it.
For a while my thoughts have been clouded
worrying if I cut you off how are you going to
feel about it,
Well I can no longer care. I have to detach to
reattach the thought process of you no longer
being here.
It's not good for me so from now on you'll see
for you I'm limiting my availability!

Gift

Life is a gift,
Your choice to enjoy it or complain about it,
But understand complaints causes time to
shorten,
While enjoyment extends,
Enjoy the present because life is a gift.

Intertwine

Have you ever made love to someone's soul not
just body?
Like really connected so strong you can feel
what they feel like it's your body?
Out of worldly, next to godly!
The shit that starts from your toes and travels
through both souls,
Each swallow of her juices quiches your thirst
making the level of desire elevate higher,
The rhythmic vibrations from the sensations of
pleasure she uncontrollably releases,
The only white flag anyone is able to throw is
what drips from the lower abyss,
No words to speak, body sweats like a leak, out
of breath I love you's that end with a kiss.

Forgiveness

5

Apologies are often used for forgiveness of
mistakes,
But constant forgiveness for repeated offenses,
Will show true colors under false pretenses.

My Flowers

Roses don't smell like daises, but I enjoy the
smell anyways,
Sunflowers are most women's favorite, and
make sunshine on a rainy day,
To know the fragrance is to receive, but what
good is it to retrieve when you are deceased?
Before I fertilize let me revitalize,
Give me flowers I can feel with my hands and
see with my eyes,
Don't wait till I'm distant and can only view
from the sky!

Impressions

Perception is what you make it,
First impressions are given once, so make sure
yours is the greatest.

For Me

You were made for me.
The way you melt to my frame everytime we
intertwine,
There is no other way to put it, the universe
dubbed you mine,
You were made for me.
The way your eyes light up the room once
they've noticed I've entered,
To the way your body quivers when I'm
journeying to your center,
You were made for me.
When you tell me it's nothing, but I can feel
something is wrong,
And how I can change your whole mode with a
intro to a song,
You were made for me.
I can show you me whole heartedly and you'll
love every piece of me,
Within you I have found my peace, that's how I
know you're made for me.

Gravity

This shift in gravity is so amazing, I'm wiser to my own amazement,

Never coming down from these feels you bring me, my charismatic charm plants you like a anchor,

I find my peace around you, your piece was missing so you built around it.

So when I feel your existence completes me, it's gravity that pulled to imperfects to perfectly complete each.

Ex-It

Attentive- ✔
Affectionate ✔
Shows interest in only me ✔
Puts me first ✔
My family and friends adore them ✔
Feels like this could be the one ✔
ring *ring*
Hello Ex-factor, you heard that to someone else I matter?
You thought you were my final but I started another chapter?
You miss your family and want to do better?
We go together like a well knit sweater?
We can work it out I don't really have someone new.
You heard I was in love, no those feelings for you,
She a good person but she just something to do,
All I ever wanted was a forever with you.

Presence

If your presence isn't appreciated,
Let them delight in your absence.

Rearview

Anything in my rear view has ran its course and
is no longer for me.
My only focus is what's ahead of me, because
anything left behind is not mine.
I was taught to take with me only what my two
arms can carry.
I carefully added your heart to my load, but you
keep attaching others to it and now the weight is
making me weary.
I have to pullover and let you go in the direction
your being pulled.
Even if it hurts this is a must, going back hinders
you, so I must go forward.
Onward to a better me.
You choose the past so I'm letting go of we.
Take care.

L.O.V.E

L-laying it all on the line and running with your
heart.
O- overcoming any and everything designed to
break the bond.
V-validating the reasons and ways to how you
feel.
E-evolving into a unbreakable union that
withstands time.

Love Is Blinding

Love is blinding, but so are black eyes.
Those same arms that hold you tight at night,
can flip like a switch and grip your neck till they
take your life.

Love is blinding, but so are bullets,
That same gun in that cabinet used to protect
your home and ones in it, can be used by the
same one you love to have your body pouring
out till no more bloods in it.

Love is blinding, but so are flashing lights,
That same set of flashing lights that you called
when you were near death on your bedroom
floor, getting punched repeatedly until you lost
consciousness are now outside your home
finally with your lover in handcuffs.

It's to late! Damn it's to late!
I thought I could control the beast I didn't know
it was succumbed by hate.

If You Allow

15

Stand up before becoming fed up,
A person will only do what you allow them to,
So if you allow them to call you "bitch" or to
strike you with a open or closed fist.
Don't get upset when no one comes to your
defense,
If you can't find the courage in yourself to stand
for self how can you expect it from someone
else?

Untitled

Everytime love comes near it ends in
catastrophe,
Starting to feel the words "I love you" are a form
of blasphemy,
One minute it's rainbows and butterflies, the
next it's b.s. covered in honey,
Captain Save another nicca bitch, but who gone
save you when he come back for his shit?,
Last month she couldn't stand him, him being
dead was her wish.
Now feelings for you a past memory while she
swallows his kids.

Thought you loved me

I thought you loved me? You said you loved
me...
But those bruises and cuts show different.
Now I'm gone and my child is alone.
Took me to long to realize you were wrong for
me.
I kept blindly wanting to see the good in WE but
you are no good for me.
I didn't think I would have to D-I-E in order to
finally S-E-E.

Better shade of green

That grass ain't greener on the other side,
Even though outside is a lovely shade of green,
the inner holds no life inside.

It's all for show and tell,
Let me show my good side and hope I disguise
the lies,

The make-up masks my ugly marks and makes
me look perfect enough for you to want me.

Now I have you hypnotized, mesmerized by lies,
wanting me more than what your used to at
home.

That grass ain't greener on the other side,
It's full of lies and pesticides.